TRUTH FOR YOUTH

NOW OR NEVER

CA RAHUL R GANDHI

Made with ♥ on the Notion Press Platform
www.notionpress.com

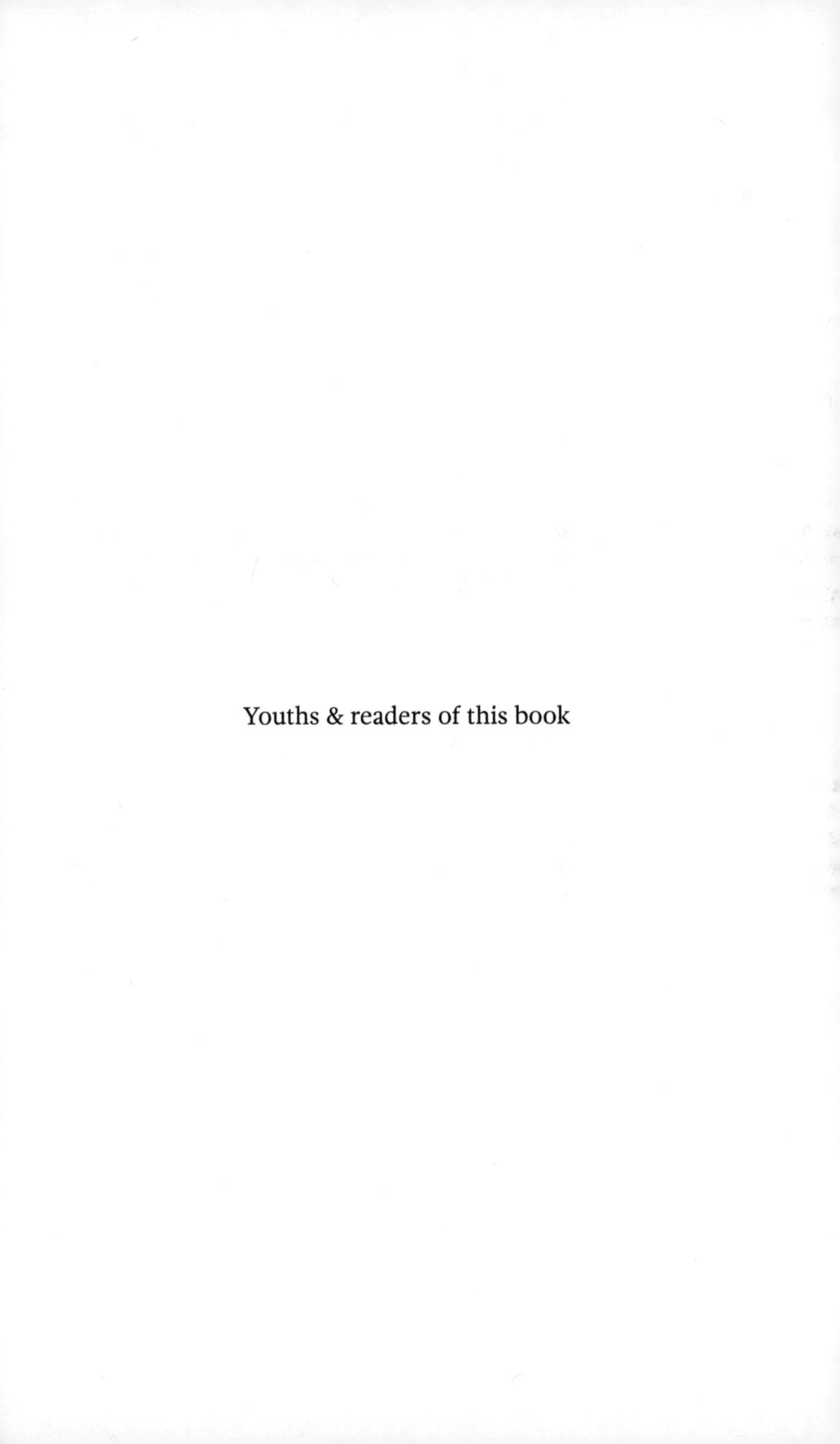

Youths & readers of this book

Contents

Contents

Preface

The idea to write this book with this type of content was shared with me by my cousins Harsha and Rishab, both of them are in the final year of their graduation. We discuss wide range of topics in our discussions and it randomly popped out that I should write a book around the various questions that are relevant to the youth of today and which can act as a framework of reference for the youth who wants to ACT on them.

Honestly speaking I have never a read book other than books relevant for my academic career until lockdown of 2020(COVID PANDEMIC). It was during this time that I started reading books and developed a keen interest towards it, wherein, I got insights on various unexplored cum explored topics which are of interest in our day-to-day life.

The content found in this book can be found in any other book or can be learnt from anyone/anywhere. I have just made an attempt to jot down few of the key points to be taken into consideration when we are given to make decision/choice. This is NOT a MOTIVATIONAL BOOK rather it's a book for those who want to take ACTION (ACT on the things) and know what is to be done when stuck in few generally faced situations.

The learnings/actions points shared in the book has its sources from my personal experiences, implementing ideas given in the books, gaining insights from the people I meet, watching movies, etc

The learnings or action points found in this book are implemented in day-to-day life and its benefits can be seen over a period of time on consistent application.

PREFACE

A book to answers HOW's of YOUTH's Life.

Acknowledgements

CA. Jeetender Jain
Ektha Surana
Booklet Team

Truth

- If teachings are not implemented within 48 hours, the possibility they being implemented in the future reduces DRASTICALLY.
- IMPLEMENTATION of an idea/habit/activity is more important than JUST KNOWING what that idea/habit/activity is.
- Be an ACTION-taking person rather than a person who just TALKS.
- The BEST investment is INVESTING IN YOURSELF.
- This is the GOLDEN Age: Make the best use of it.
- Neither MONEY alone NOR Knowledge alone can give you a complete view. But the right mixture of KNOWLEDGE and MONEY will help you have a holistic view of your life.
- Acquiring knowledge will help you have clarity; and with clarity & requisite skills (put together) you have the art with which you can convince any person and gain their trust/confidence.
- If you wish to GROW in any aspect of your LIFE, then FIRST STEP is to '**MEASURE**' where you are standing currently.
- To rethink on the decision is your strength also and weakness too. So just do exactly what is needed.
- I believe that things explained with LOGIC backed by SCIENCE are better than any RANDOM way of explaining. Thereby, we can still make decisions without following any of the methods/ideologies that are recommended in the book. But if we do follow, we might get holistic and greater perspective is what I believe.

This book is not edited by professional editor's, we would appreciate if you bring to our notice on any edits to be made by writing to us on gandhirahul511@gmail.com

So, let's start with few of the question faced by today Youth's *(like me and you)* and how to make decisions for YOURSELF in a WISE Way.

CHAPTER ONE

Decision Making Process

As an individual we are bombarded with various decisions to be made every now and then, in this process, we take many decisions without even we noticing that we are deciding on them. But, when the time to take a crucial decision comes, we are stuck and try to make that decision too spontaneously, wherein, we are thinking about various possible inputs and outputs for a particular situation.

Therefore, there are two choices i.e., either bluntly follow what we think or we can APPLY logical steps to make an informed decision.

- Steps for taking an informed decision:
  - **Step 1:** Data collection
  - **Step 2:** Transforming the data in the understandable format
  - **Step 3:** Correlation/Check with your intention/needs
  - **Step 4:** Then Decide

- Most of the times just writing things on the piece of paper gives immense CLARITY and UNDERSTANDING. Just try this and see the results for yourself!!

Note: Before taking any decision ONLY collect facts/ data ***i.e.,*** Before decision date DON'T take any decision

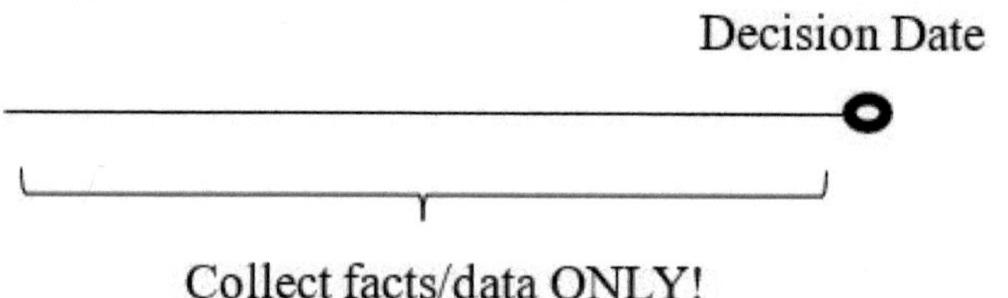

CHAPTER TWO

How to Choose the Right Career?

Choice of career is one of the most crucial decisions in everyone's life. I have come across many such instances and have also personally experienced that the career is almost decided based on what our friends or family members recommend as the best career.

There are various career counselling sessions and other modes out in the market. But taking your own decisions will make you more mature cum knowledgeable and remember that ***'there is no one better than yourself to DECIDE for YOURSELF'.***

I would like you to decide the right career for yourself in a logic manner. The below are the recommended steps that can be followed.

Wouldn't it be great if the CAREER you choose ALIGNS with your REQUIREMENTS?

The First and the foremost step would be write done your REQUIREMENTS *(what you expect from the course/*

career). Few of your requirement can be:

- *I want to be happy?*
- *I want to make a living out of it?*
- *I want to be satisfied and content with it?*

Thereafter the below steps would help us,

- **Step 1: CAREER/COURSE OPTIONS** - List down all the possible career options that come to your mind and talking to your elders, friends and colleagues and what the search engine recommends. Few of the career options are listed below for your quick reference
    - Bachelor course
    - Master's course
    - Professional course
    - Influencer
    - Make-up Artist
    - Certified Yoga Trainer
    - Dietician
    - Interior Designer
    - Dancer / Singer
    - Actor/ Actress/ Writer/ Choreography
- **Step 2: PRELIMINARY ELIMINATION PROCESS** - Read out the basic information about each of courses listed in Step 1 to get a fair idea that if you would be interested in it.

  "Basis the preliminary research filter out the courses/career that are don't align with your

requirement."

- **Step 3: GET the insights from EXPERIENCED** - Meet the **4 types** of people in each of the above shortlisted career stream.
    - **Type 1:** Your colleague who wants to pursue this shortlisted career
    - **Type 2:** Fresher who is in the last year of the said course
    - **Type 3:** Person who has 5 years of experience in the field
    - **Type 4:** Person who has more than 20 years of experience in that field.
- **Step 4: OWN RESEARCH** - Carryout your own research about each of the career.
- **Step 5: RATING** - Based on the data and information gathered by you, please rate each career option against each of your requirements on a scale of 1 to 10.
- **Step 6: KNOW the RESULTS** - Do the total of these factors. Just to have a fair estimate if you still want this career.

"***There is one more possible way wherein, you keep eliminating the options which you don't want and then reach to the ultimate career/ course for you.***

By following the above approach, at the end you can comfortably say to yourself that I decided the right course/career for myself based on all the resources available with me at that POINT in time"

ACTIVITY

I have tabulated a small table below for quick understanding and reference.

Name:

Date & Day:

Signature:

Sr.No	YOUR requirement/expectation from Course/Career	WHY is THIS your requirement/expectation?
1		
2		
3		
..		

Sr.No	Career Options Available	Your requirements					Total
		1	2	3	.	.	
1	Option 1						
2	Option 2						
3	Option 3						
...	...						

DECIDE FOR YOURSELF or FOLLOW OTHER.

You get to CHOOSE!!

CHAPTER THREE

HOW TO CHOOSE THE RIGHT LIFE PARTNER?

Having a right life partner means getting married in India. Marriage in itself is a choice which has both pros and cons. It is upto a particular individual if he wants to have a life partner or not. Suppose an individual decides to have a life partner then at the root cause he is looking for a person who is 'UNDERSTANDING & CARING'. Yes, this is the one-line answer 'UNDERSTANDING & CARING' for having a right life partner. Simple right!!

However, I have tried to break this down in a logical manner to get more clarity which can help us in taking a wise decision for ourselves. Trying to answer the below questions will help you in this process:

Step 1: Understanding the other person.

Step 2: Understanding yourself.

} Just data collection DON'T take any decision.

Step 3: Decision (Yes/No... how much percentage)

Now, let us dig deep into each of these steps

- **Step 1: How to understand the other person**
    - Be **genuinely interested** in the other person and try to explore everything possible. The basic things can be about their education, expectations, family, cousins, happy moments, etc
    - Know about their **'Likes vs Dislikes'** on small matters to big matters.
    - Know about their **'Wants vs Don't wants'** on small matters to big matters.
    - Know about their **personal traits** like
        - Are they generally Lazy or Enthusiastic?
        - Do they celebrate their happy moments? If yes, then how?
        - How do they deal with sad moments?
        - What do they do when they feel boring?
        - What do they do when they are angry/frustrated?
        - How do they get irritated? ....etc
    - Know about their **attitude?**
        - What is his/her attitude towards Life?
        - What is his/her attitude towards himself/herself?
        - What is his/her attitude towards peers?
        - What is his/her attitude towards others (can be family members/ relatives)? ....etc
    - Know about the importance of few **factors** like

    - How important is health? *(Post pandemic health has gained importance like never before)*
    - It can be mental health, physical health, emotional health or spiritual health?
    - Priorities in life? ....etc

- **Step 2: How to understand yourself in the present situation**

  - Answers the same question for yourself as in Step 1 and make a note of it in a piece of paper.
  - Know clearly about your Wants (expectations, if any) Vs Don't Wants

- **Step 3: DECIDE for YOURSELF**

  - ARE YOU "**OK**" with 'the' other person? *i.e.,*

    - Their Wants (expectations, if any) Vs Don't wants?
    - Their Likes Vs Dis-likes?
    - Their Personal traits?
    - Their Attitude?Other Factors?

Then **two** possible answers

1. If No, then need not go ahead with that person as a life partner
2. If Yes, then how much percentage? Say 70% then remaining 30% are you OK to deal with it? If yes, then Congratulations – you found your partner BUT WAIT FOR THE OTHER PERSON TO CONFIRM ON THE SAME

- ◦ Diagrammatic representation for ease of understanding

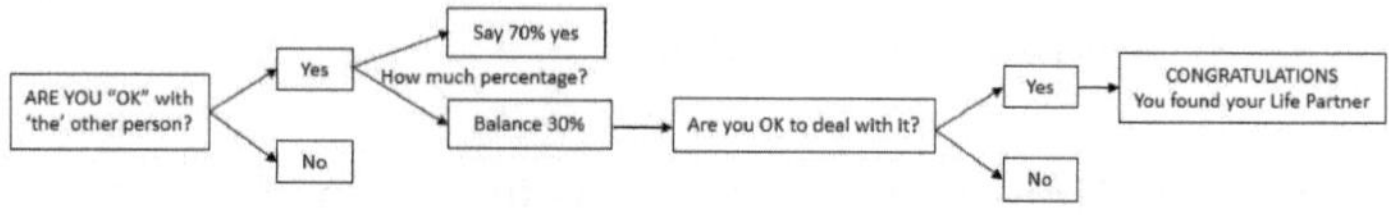

- Is the other person **OK with 'you' being their life partner? - Yes**
- Are you ready to spend the rest of your life with that person WITHOUT expecting any change *i.e.,* Accepting as they are now? – Yes

If the Answer to the above 3 questions is **'Yes'**. Then CONGRATULATIONS from my SIDE and *HAPPY LEADING A LIFE OF JOYFULLNESS & HAPPINESS!!*

Note: Human psychology & few lessons/facts

- Things come in PACKAGE!! You can't expect everything from a single person.
- Never take the other person for granted.
- At the core every human being wants to be
    - RESPECTED
    - ACCEPTED as they are
    - RECOGNISED at regular intervals
- **Considering the INDIAN SOCIETY:** It is Girl who leaves her home and stays with the guy. Girl is not only marrying the guy but also accepting his family more

than anyone else. If the boy wishes to stay with his parents and other family members, post marriage then in that case it is very important to note that whenever a GIRL is communicating about anything it implies that she is not only communicating to GUY but also HIS FAMILY (It is boy's duty to see to it that Girl's requirements matches with the Family requirements). A Girl might not explicitly communicate this but it's implied that GUY will understand this for her.

- The decision about the finance is best made with the use of EXCEL tool. The decision about the Human is best made with the use of HEART.
- Be happy that you get to decide for yourself because most of them aren't that lucky enough.

CHAPTER FOUR

HOW TO HAVE A HOLISTIC OR 360 DEGREE VIEW/ APPROACH TO ANYTHING IN LIFE/BUSINESS?

Do you agree that all of us will choose different things in life?

Wouldn't you be happy if you get 360-degree perspective of what you chose? This would not only empower your choice but also make you confident cum knowledgeable.

Do you agree if what we see in VR is better than any 2D/3D pictures? VR helps us to see/view all surroundings too. Answering these questions will help you to VR view. Hahaha!!

BAD analogy but it's TRUE!!

Therefore, to get 360 degree or holistic perspective, you just need to do one thing ***i.e.,***

'Answer 5W and 1H'

Let's understand what it means:

Answer **WHY** you chose to do this? – this will help you find the PURPOSE;

Answer **WHO** will do it? -- this will help you find the PERSON;

Answer **WHAT** will be done? -– this will help you find the OUTCOME;

Answer **WHEN** it will be done? -– this will help you find the TIME PERIOD;

Answer **WHERE** it will be done? -– this will help you find the PLACE; and

Answer **HOW** it will be done? - this will help you find the PROCESS/PROCEDURE.

CHAPTER FIVE

HOW TO GET CLARITY OF ANYTHING IN LIFE/BUSINESS?

Having clarity of what we do is like having strong foundation. Clarity is also different levels. I genuinely believe that if you have highest level of clarity then you don't need any motivation from external stimulus to do that action.

Also, given that in today's world we have so much information, having clarity in itself acts as a super power and gives us an edge.

So, the question is how do achieve this highest-level of clarity? Again, you just do this one thing ***i.e.,***

'Ask 5 times why to yourself?'

Let's understand what it means:

Say you want to do this thing A.

1. **Why** do you want to do thing A? because reason is 'B'
2. **Why** is the reason 'B'? because reason is 'C'
3. **Why** is the reason 'C'? because reason is 'D'
4. **Why** is the reason 'D'? because reason is 'E'
5. **Why** is the reason thing E? .....

Illustration: Say you want to do YOGA

1. Why do you want to do YOGA? because I want to be 'Fit'
2. Why do you want to be 'Fit'? because I want to travel/look good....etc
3. Why do you want to travel/look good....etc? because I want to....so on...

At end of 5th WHY you will have immense clarity.

Now, you can CONGRATULATE yourself that you have BETTER CLARITY than before.

Note: Write down the answers in a piece of paper. Doing this will act as validation and will build your confidence behind taking any particular decision.

CHAPTER SIX

How to get Clarity and Holistic view? (Combination of the above two techniques)

Applying the technique of **'5W & 1H'** with **'5 WHY'** will give you insights, confidence, knowledge...etc that you could have missed.

You won't be distracted by what other say or do. This is because you have clarity and 360- degree view of what you chose to do.

TRY to apply and see the results by yourself.

Pictorial representation

CHAPTER SEVEN

HOW TO CONNECT TO NATURE?

NATURE has been wonderful gift to all of us. One of the most wonderful thing about nature is its '**impermanence**' nature *.i.e.,* it teaches us that Change is the only thing which is constant. Sometimes change is fast and sometimes change is very slow to be noticed by our normal senses.

Most of us are on various social media platforms like Instagram, snapchat, facebook, etc. We all very often see our connections and advertisements posting pictures of mother NATURE and its beauty. In these cases, we all see pictures and connect to NATURE's beauty visually. But trust me visiting nature has its own merits.

Suppose you plan to VISIT to any of such places, in such a case, how to TAKE this experience of yourself CONNECTING to nature NEXT LEVEL?

Follow these **4 steps** to do so:

- **Step 1: Visually via Eye**

  - Visually watch the nature and its constantly changing. *(Highly active sense here is 'EYE')*

- **Step 2: Close your Eyes**

  - This indirectly increases the activity of your ears. Thereby you hear the sound of nature. *(Highly active sense here is 'EAR')*

- **Step 3: Close your Eyes & block your EARS with your fingers so that sound doesn't enter the ears**

  - This indirectly increases the activity of your nose. Thereby you can feel the fragrance of the nature. *(Highly active sense here is 'NOSE')*

- **Step 4: Touch**

  - Touch the nearby surrounding and feel its vibrations. Experience the fresh air of the NATURE.*(Highly active sense here is 'TOUCH')*

Try this out, maybe you might gain something meaningful & insightful, thereby, taking your experience to totally next level. *(Tip: Spend a minimum of 30 seconds to 1 minutes at each step)*

ACTIVITY

Visit the same place in different seasons and get to experience this fact.

CHAPTER EIGHT

HOW TO UNDERSTAND THE OPPOSITE GENDER?

This has been an age-old question and there are many of them giving different perspectives to it. I came across a book named 'MEN ARE FROM MARS and WOMEN ARE FROM VENUS'. I personally recommended this book in this context.

Nevertheless, I have tried to put up few psychological factors in understanding opposite gender as below:

- Appreciate the fact that MEN and WOMEN are DIFFERENT, in the sense that, both might use the same words, but they mean completely different meaning.
- Men and women need to remember that the emotional needs of the opposite sex are not the same as their own. Providing our partners with the wrong type of emotional needs will not be greatly appreciated.

- Communication between partners should be loving and respectful; verbal attacks by contrast are highly destructive. It is often not what you say that matters but how you say it that makes/breaks the relationship.
- The energy required to flourish the relationship is same as energy required to destroy it. So, you get to choose where you need to spend that energy and what memories you would like to carry from it.

I have tried to put in a comparative for ease of understanding:

<u>**Characteristics of MEN**</u>

1. MEN are generally solution providers. Therefore, when the other person communicates him something he generally tries to provide solution.
2. MEN need answer only when they specifically ask for it.
3. When faced with tough problems, MEN generally figure out the solution by themselves by going into their own caves (turn silent and inward) where they want minimum or no interaction from anyone. Hence, MEN are non-communicative and non-expressive so that they can work out how best they can offer help themselves.
4. Men demand the right to be free from time to time. Therefore, when a man feels free, he finds it easier to support woman's need to be heard
5. **Scoring:** In MEN's dictionary it is presumed that if he does some BIG things then all rest of the small things will be taken care of.

<u>**Characteristics of WOMEN**</u>

1. WOMEN wants to be HEARD. They don't expect SOLUTIONS.
2. WOMEN providing solution out of her care is generally not appreciated due to this psychological difference.
3. When faced with tough problems, WOMEN just wants her partner to listen to it and not provide any solution as such. Hence, WOMEN are generally communicative and expressive so that they can work out how best they can offer help themselves.
4. Women demand the right to be heard from time to time. Therefore, when a woman feels heard she finds it easier to support a man's need to be free
5. **Scoring:** In WOMEN's dictionary it is all counted as ONE tick (doesn't matter if MEN do SMALL or BIG thing to impress/express women all of them are counted as one tick irrespective of the magnitude)

Please note that the characteristics named here of MEN can be exhibited by WOMEN and vice versa.

Each of above can be explained in detail with practical examples but that's not the intention of this book. Just reflect on these differences then you will be in a better position to understand the opposite gender, thereby, you can act accordingly.

CHAPTER NINE

HOW TO GET YOURSELF IN BEST HEALTH?

Health has gained tremendous importance in the youths due to youth icons like Virat Kohli, lesson learnt from COVID PANDEMIC, etc. While there are youths who focus only on physical wellbeing or mental wellbeing. Hence it is important to be get overall perspective of HEALTH.

For me, HEALTH is divided into FOUR AREAS where we have to focus and take actions to improve i.e.,

1. Financial health,
2. Physical Health,
3. Emotional health, and
4. Spiritual health.

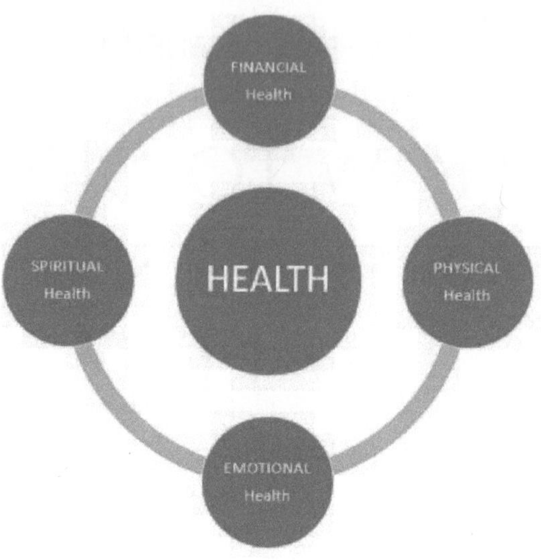

Pictorial representation

Each of these is interrelated with other whether directly or indirectly. Focusing on one area will automatically help you develop your health in other areas.

CHAPTER TEN

HOW TO PLAN YOUR GROWTH?

In our school life or professional courses or professional life our growth is pre-decided, wherein, you will be promoted from level 1 to level 2 in one/two years (here growth is inherent part of it). But when we look at our life as a whole, it is we who are in charge of our life and hence we are responsible to plan our GROWTH (without this growth factor life would seem to like dimming). Do you agree if we plan growth in our health then automatically, we are planning growth for our life? So, how do we plan our growth for life?

- Here are the quick action steps for you
    - **Step 1:** MEASURE where you are standing in each of these 4 areas of Health
    - **Step 2:** DECIDE where you want to reach in each of these areas.
    - **Step 3:** FORMULATE an action plan about it.
    - **Step 4:** ACT on it.

(Kindly refer the activity for ready template)

- For the purpose of action, I would recommend using **'20-20-20 Rule' CONSISTENTLY** wherein everyday 1 hour is required to be spent as follows
    - **First 20 minutes** – MOVE - Do a PHYSICAL ACTIVITY in a way that you get sweat from your body.
    - **Next 20 minutes** – REFLECT - Sit with yourself focusing on your breathe/write a gratitude journal
    - **Final 20 minutes** – GROWTH - Read a book / Listen to PODCAST. (*This rule is from the book named '5 AM Club'.)*

ACTIVITY

I have tabulated a small table below for quick understanding and reference.

Name:
Date & Day:
Signature:

Action plan report

Particular	Financial Health	Physical Health	Emotional Health	Spiritual Health
Current state				
Goal to be achieved				
Action to be taken				

Bonus

- Every year plan your growth in these 4 areas and add at least 1 new skill.
- Choose a sport and increase your level of competence in that sport *(it can be any sport like cricket, football, volleyball, badminton, squash, tennis, swimming...etc)*

Chose any new HABIT/SKILL you want to ADD, then start spending undivided 20 minutes a day on it for next 21 days. If you like it, then you can take it forward or else you can try something else.

CHAPTER ELEVEN

HOW TO SPEND YOUR TIME?

How you spend your time almost determines everything you do personally and professionally. But still, we hardly keep a track of how we spend time over day/week/month/year. Without changing how you spend your time, you can't expect any change in the results you achieve.

- One of the most important learning from my CA journey and my life till now is **'RESPECT TIME with full honor or else time won't respect you'.**

    - *Time is one thing which comes for 'free of cost' but it is 'Priceless' (time in itself is an oxymoron). Own your time for your own wellbeing.*
    - *You should be knowing where you are spending time, how much time are you spending, how much time you actually need to spend and how to steal time for more important things in life.*

- The most wonderful thing about TIME is you can't WASTE it in ADVANCE. You might have WASTED your past but the FUTURE is still in your HANDS.

- Below is the small table that will help you analyze if you are spending your time correctly.

	URGENT	NOT URGENT
IMPORTANT	**Quadrant I** *Things which are urgent & important* **DO**	**Quadrant II** *Things which are NOT urgent & important* **PLAN**
NOT IMPORTANT	**Quadrant III** *Things which are Urgent & NOT important* **DELEGATE**	**Quadrant IV** *Things which are NOT urgent & NOT important* **ELIMINATE or AVOID**

"Ideally you should be spending most of your time in Quadrant II which represents things/activities which are important but not urgent which includes your physical fitness, your time-off, etc"

ACTIVITY

I have tabulated a small table below for quick understanding and reference.

Date:

Sr. No	Tasks	Priority	Quadrant 1/2/3/4	Re-prioritize
1				
2				
3				

Step 1: Write down the list of task/activities you want to do for a particular time period.

Step 2: Prioritize the tasks starting from high priority to low priority with
1 - High Priority
2 -
N - Least priority

Step 3: Classify the tasks in Column 2 basis the matrix in the previous page into Quadrant 1/2/3/4.

Step 4: Reprioritize the tasks in column by comparing Step 2 & Step 3. i.e.

Quadrant 2 – Highest Priority

Quadrant 1 – High

Quadrant 3 – Low

Quadrant 4 - Lowest

NOTE: *Once you allocate your time in the above manner and work on it consistently over a period the time. Then you see start seeing a drastic change in your routine.*

CHAPTER TWELVE

HOW TO RESPOND TO YOUR EMOTIONS?

Do you agree that the way we respond to a situation almost creates an impression in the other person's mind on the kind of person we are?

Again, most of the times we just REACT to a situation instead of even trying to know the possible options that are available with us. This REACTION has both pros and cons. Now, lets us take ourselves one-step ahead and see with an open mind on what are the possible options with us in ANY SITUATION.

- Any situation you always have 4 alternatives available for your disposable *i.e.*,

4 A's

1. **You can AVOID that situation**
2. **You can ALTER that situation**
3. **You can ADAPT to that situation**
4. **You can ACCEPT to that situation**

Pictorial representation

NOTE

- It is always beneficial to RESPOND to any situation instead of REACTING.

- Don't exaggerate any situation in your mind. See things AS THEY ARE.

WORRY/ FEAR/ANXIETY

- Very often we all worry about different things. Let's learn how to deal with Worry Just ask this one question to yourself
    - Can you do something about it?
        - If YES – then why Worry (means you can ACT on the situation and therefore WHY WORRY)
        - If NO – then why Worry (means factors are not in your control and therefore WHY WORRY) *(This is from the book 'Life's Amazing Secrets'.)*

Pictorial representation

- If you are worrying about many things, then start with **one worry at the time** instead of thinking of all the worries together. Even sand granular from an hour glass falls one at a time then why to think of all the worries together.
- Go on a walk or do an **intense workout**. Basically, the idea is that Mind stops thinking of that situation for now.
- Most often we worry that

  - What if this happens? How will I deal with this? Who will I approach? Will someone help me?
  - In such case we are thinking about the various outcomes if that situation arises i.e., We are thinking in terms of **possibility**.
  - In such a case **'replace POSSIBILITY with PROBABILITY'.** Just doing this might reduce the intensity of your worry.

- WRITING on the **piece of a paper** about your worry.

ANGRY/SADNESS

In most of the cases, what makes us angry is that person did this thing or he said this thing. It is obvious that we can't control what the other person says/does BUT how to respond to such a situation is totally at our OWN Choice.

*Remember that **'Anger is the punishment that you give to yourself for someone else's mistake'***

Here are few tips to help you in such a situation:

- When someone does anything to you which makes you angry, then just ignore the situation laughing.
- SMILE;
- LAUGHTER is the best Medicine;
- Let your ACTIONS speak instead of your WORDS;
- Give your self-time may be overnight, day or two and then rethink. TRUST me the response you decided to give at that moment will be different from the response you propose to give after the break.

HAPPYNESS/JOYFULLNESS

Celebrate smallest of the success/achievements with yourself, person in your close circles. Celebration can be through a party, taking our circle for lunch....etc

Doing this releases dopamine in the brain and instigates us to do more of such thing in future from a neuroscience perspective.

CHAPTER THIRTEEN

HOW TO CHOOSE YOUR FRIENDS CIRCLE?

Believe it or not - the choice of our friends influences our decision and the way we lead whether directly or indirectly.

BUT does it mean you should not be friends with people who don't align? The answer to this question is BIG NO!!

I would rather say have ALL kind of friends, interact with them, LEARN from them, try to view the world/things from their perspective, etc. This is broadening your horizon to an altogether DIFFERENT LEVEL!

Thereafter, GIVE more time to those whom you feel connected and confident to share things with. If there is NONE then its fine because you always have YOURSELF!!

Below is the small analogy where you are in the middle of all the circles. First one/two circles represent things which only you know and you want no one else to know about it *(this will help you to keep few things in private which no one will know other than you)*. Each circle represents how close a person is to you and based on this what you would like to share with him. Each of your friend/relative/family members may fall under any of these circles and depending on it you share the things/thoughts/feelings with them.

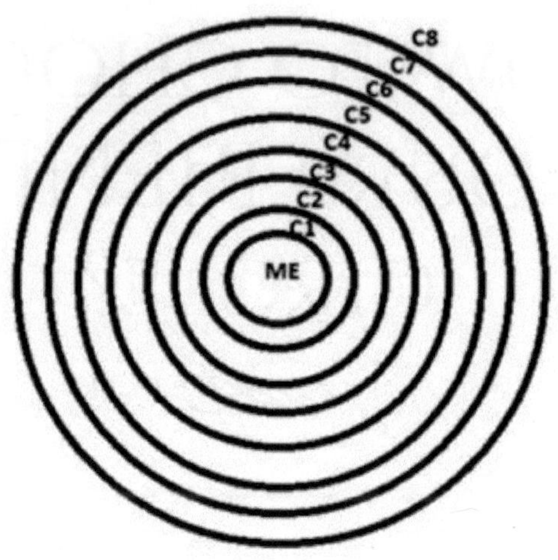

Pictorial representation

Caution: The kind of ACTIVITIES you want to indulge along with your friends is upto to you. So, choose wisely if you still want to do those activities!

CHAPTER FOURTEEN

HOW TO SPEND MONEY?

Generally, we don't have any structured approach for spending money. We spend money on the things which we like. When faced with a decision whether to buy a product/service, the notion is Yes, lets buy it because we have money.

Here is a simple rule which we all can use to ***spend money prudently.*** The rule requires you to answer these simple set of questions:

- Is it my NECESSICITY?
- Will it increase my HEALTH?
- Will it increase my WEALTH?
- Will it increase my KNOWLEDGE?
- Will it help in increase RELATIONSHIP?
- Will it give me an ENRICHING EXPERIENCE?

If the answer to any of these questions is YES, then CONGRATULATIONS you can spend money on it.

NOTE 1: SPENDING varies with whose money, is it?

Most of us are generally dependent on the parents, while, few of us also are independent. The money earned by yourself can be spent the way you want.

Suppose you want to purchase an i-Phone! Or You want to go to foreign country for a trip!

YES, you can PROVIDED it's YOU who has earned the money after providing for your family needs, if any.

NO, if the money belongs to your parents. *(It can be YES if your parents allow it assuming that it's REASONABLE and the FINANCIAL Health of the family allows it)*

NOTE 2: Relationship with money?

Each of us come from different FINANCIAL background. Many of us are from middle class family, while, there are a few from rich family and a few of from Poor family.

People from Rich family should NOT be having an EGO that they have a car/iPhone, etc. RATHER they can be grateful that I have this. THERE is LOT of difference between the both!

CHAPTER FIFTEEN

EDUCATE YOURSELF WITH REAL FINANCE?

We all will be going out to make our living by earning MONEY. TRUE!!

If I just ask you one question *i.e.,*

"***What are the uses of MONEY?*** "

Possibly you will answer many things. Here is an attempt to ease it.

Below are the 5 USES of money to have ***balanced cum harmonious*** relations with it

1. To provide for NECESSITIES
2. To secure near future with SAVINGS
3. To provide for our ENJOYMENT
4. To INVESTMENT
5. To Contribute to the SOCIETY (i.e., Charity)

When you earn money and know the purpose of it, it will help you know why you are earning money and where to spend money.

REAL FINANCE in itself is a huge topic for discussion cum application in our day-to-day life. Here, I would just give you two tips *i.e.*,

1. **BUY REAL ASSETS**

- REAL ASSETS are the one which GENERATE CASHFLOW.

> *"(Assets have been defined in accounts, Income tax, GST...etc. but never forget what REAL ASSET is)"*

> *"**Eg:** Buying a car is not an asset unless it generates cashflow for us."*

2. **70:20:10 Rule (ELR RULE)**

- Follow the above rule to repay your liability and BUILD REAL ASSETS for your financial wellness.

> *"Say your earnings is 100 then,*
>
> - *Maximum **Expense** should be restricted to 70% of your earnings (i.e., 100*70%= 70)*
> - ***Loans/Liability,** if any is to be repaid at 20% of your earnings (i.e., 100*20%= 20)*
> - *Minimum **real assets** should be 10% of your earnings (i.e., 100*10%= 10)*

CHAPTER SIXTEEN

How to keep HIGH FOCUS on your GOAL?

FOCUS is more important than anything in today's era. With abundance of choices, so many things are available that can distract us on a single click of button *(of course it depends on how we use it)*. So how do we keep focus on our GOALS and get less distracted?

- There is this one thing we can do. Do we ever forget to wear our clothes? No right. Then let's not forget our dreams/goals. Hence you can make the best use of this knowledge by following

ONE SIMPLE STEP

STICK a PAPER on the CLOSET from where you get your clothes. Every time you wear your clothes you will know what you want to do and what you are born for.

- When there are too many tasks/things to do and not understanding where to start then, chose any ONE task and USE POMODORO TECHNIQUE wherein you will be required to give 25 minutes of your undivided attention to it.
- 'MULTITASKING is a myth. Rather we all do SWITCHTASKING and give it the name of MULTITASKING'. At a given point of time we can do one activity and when we take frame of time, we keep switching from one activity to another. Therefore, FOCUS on ONE activity you are doing at that point-in-time rather than multiple.
- Everyone has their OWN STRENGTH. If you keep focussing on other's strengths then you might NOT even see yours, recognize and work on your strengths. Therefore, it is always beneficial to FOCUS on your strength instead of OTHERS. Doing this will BUILD your CONFIDENCE and empower you with STRENGTH.
- We should either COMPLETELY believe in OURSELVES 'OR' COMPLETELY believe in SUPREME ENERGY i.e., a force greater than you. But in actual sense our belief system keeps toggling between energy and ourselves. Keep a watch on it to reflect upon it.

> "*Believing in supreme energy would NOT mean that everything will be done by the supreme energy RATHER it means supreme energy will 'come for your rescue or show the right direction' and work for you ONLY when you too go and work for what you want.*"

CHAPTER SEVENTEEN

How to use Social Media Smartly?

Social media giants have understood the psychology and neurology of the human being in much better way than any other industry and using it in the best possible way. I have one question you should ask yourself i.e.

> "*Isn't it true that 'You should OWN an electronic device & electronic device should NOT OWN YOU?'*"

If YES, below are a few tips which will help you save your time and use electronic device smartly to your advantage.

- Switch off the notification option in the social media application: This will help you to access it when you want to access it and not when they want you to use it;
- Create a no-phone zone in the home wherein if the members are coming to that place, then no phones are

to be used. This detaches us from the device for a while and provides us an opportunity to talk to each other, which, in turn increases our bond with that member/ person.

- Don't keep phone near you when you are sleeping. This increases the quality of sleep and refreshes you more. You can also use normal alarm clock near your bed instead of alarm in the phone.

ACTIVITY

Switch on the screen timer on for a week on your mobile device and check

- How many hours per day are you spending on the mobile device?
- Which are the applications you are spending on?

Evaluate yourself if it's worth spending that much time on that particular application/device.

Bonus

- Watch documentary on Netflix named 'The Social Dilemma'.
- Consume content about this topic from books, social media and your friends/peers.

CHAPTER EIGHTEEN

HOW TO HAVE RIGHT MINDSET?

Human mind and its evolution over the period of time is the KEY factor for our existence and growth till date. Having said that, we can say that the type of mindset you carry is directly proportional to the level of joyfulness and the attitude you carry towards your own life.

Basis the above, you have CHOICE on what is the kind of mindset you want to carry with yourself. I have tried to note a few of the mindset which I think we can have:

- You have to decide/choose for yourself, you can't blame someone else for your decision.*(Implementing just this one thing will help you to take ownership of your life)*
- Be an ACTION taking person rather than a person who just talks;
- Have a GROWTH mindset in all the areas of your life;
- Have an ABUNDANCE, OPPORTUNISTIC & OPTIMISTIC mindset;
- Always having learning attitude and accepting the fact that there are many things that you don't know;

- In SUCCESS there is no full stops, we only have commas. SUCCESS is a JOURNEY and NOT a DESTINATION.
- Always have below three things with you

CURIOSITY of a CHILD,
ENERGY of an ADULT, and
NECESSITY/WISDOM of OLD PERSON!!

Action points you can take

- Don't take any DECISIONS when you are SAD and Don't make any PROMISES when you are HAPPY;
- EXPRESS Gratitude to at least one person a DAY
- Do the RIGHT thing instead of the EASY thing. It's a difficult choice but it leads to the CORRECT path!!
- The KEY to GROWTH lies in your DAILY ROUTINE. It is not a one long activity of say 21 hours rather it's an activity of 1 hour every day for next 21 days.
- Celebrate smallest of the things/win and stay in that moment;
- Negotiate in a manner that it's a WIN – WIN deal/ situation;
- Focus on the Process and the results will follow. Be IMPATIENT with the PROCESS and PATIENT with the RESULTS!
- Revisiting your growth journey at regular intervals. The interval period of 3 months can be good enough.
- Never fix a frame of reference (JUDGE) for a person. If you do so then you will miss out on the learning that the other person might share which is relevant to you i.e., be open to change from the other person.

- You could have been studious in school or may be not, it doesn't matter BUT what matters is that 'CAN YOU LEAD a LIFE that you be PROUD OFF!!'

CHAPTER NINETEEN

STORY: WISHES COME TRUE!!

Hi Pals,

Today instead of a story let me tell you a real incident! The incident which I heard from my grandparents and still stays in my heart afresh.

I will take you through an Indian Village named 'Govvankoppa'. Amongst the many of the village people living, there were 2 best friends (Gopi and Mani).

Both Gopi and Mani were equal in all the sense be it studies, family, sports, education, finance or any other field of life. They both were considered to be richest person in the villages and both of them had equal wealth. (Note that wealth is something which everyone wants to have as much as possible whether knowingly or unknowingly.)

Every morning, they got up and prayed to the God in a very humble way. God was very impressed by both and asked them individually to ask for one thing ('Only one thing') they want in life and he would grant it.s

Gopi said, "God make me such a person that I am always getting money". Mani said, "God make me such person that I am always giving money".

God blessed them and said with a smiling face that all your wishes shall come true. After a period of 5 years when I visited this village, I was surprised to see this.

What was I surprised about?

Did Gopi surpass Mani in wealth? Or

Did Mani surpass Gopi in wealth? Or

Were both equal in wealth?

"*After 5 years................*"

Over the 5 years, Gopi had lost all his wealth, his family members abandoned him and had lost all the respect in the village

Now, Gopi was begging at every house in the village for money, so that he can eat food and Mani was the wealthiest person in the village and was still donating 'a lot and lot of his wealth'.

(Remember that Gopi's wish was that he always gets money and his wish had come true wherein, he was always getting money.

Mani's wish was that he always wanted to give back to society and his wish too had come true. He was the wealthiest person, donating a lot of money and living a happy and healthy life)

What's the learning we can take from this incident?

'Always have a cause to serve the society, rest everything will happen'

Now it's up to you if you want to be Gopi or Mani.

So 'Choose Wisely'

Key Take Aways And Action Plan

3 Learnings from the book

1.
2.
3.

ONLY ONE Action you propose to take

You can reachout to the author atgandhirahul511@gmail.com

LinkedIn: https://www.linkedin.com/in/ca-rahul-r-gandhi-19a777136

Instagram ID: the_chartered_guy

Printed by Libri Plureos GmbH in Hamburg,
Germany

9 798889 868699